Donovan & Winslow
in
Obey Your Parents

by:

Mr. A with Angela

ISBN: 978-1480258631

Library of Congress Control Number: 2011911496

Printed in the United States of America

Dedicated to my parents Aubrey and Lillian
for whom I am most thankful.

SEE WHAT I MEAN DONOVAN, WHY ARE YOUR MOM AND DAD SO MEAN?

THEY'RE NOT BEING MEAN WINSLOW, MOM AND DAD KNOW WHAT'S BEST FOR ME.

BUT DONOVAN, I KNOW WHAT'S GOOD TOO. SEE WHAT I MEAN, WHY NOT LISTEN TO ME?

MMM, MMM, MMM, WHAT TO DO WINSLOW...
WE MUST OBEY OUR PARENTS AND LISTEN TO THEM. IT WILL KEEP US OUT OF TROUBLE.

I HELP MY PARENTS BY PICKING UP MY TOYS OFF THE FLOOR, MAKING MY BED AND FEEDING MY DOG TITO.

MOM, I'M FINISHED WITH MY CHORES. MAY I GO PLAY AT WINSLOW'S HOUSE?

YES DONOVAN, ONLY IF YOU ARE FINISHED.

GOOD JOB DONOVAN!
I AM SO PROUD OF YOU. I'VE BAKED SOME
COOKIES FOR ALL YOUR HARD WORK.

Obey Your Parents

Obey Your Parents

Obey Your Parents

LET'S PLAY CATCH WITH MY NEW BALL!

Obey Your Parents

OH NO! WHERE IS MY BALL? I CAN'T FIND IT.

MY MOM AND DAD TOLD ME TO CLEAN UP MY ROOM BUT THAT'S NO FUN.

MMM, MMM, MMM WHAT TO DO. COME ON WINSLOW. YOU MUST OBEY YOUR PARENTS. LET'S PUT THESE TOYS AWAY AND LOOK FOR YOUR NEW BALL.

SEE WINSLOW, YOUR ROOM LOOKS SO MUCH BETTER NOW.

Obey Your Parents

WINSLOW, MY MOM SAID FOR ME TO BE HOME BY 6 O' CLOCK. I MUST OBEY HER AND GO HOME AT ONCE.

Obey Your Parents

Obey Your Parents

EVERYONE, WE MUST "OBEY OUR PARENTS" FOR THEY KNOW WHAT'S BEST FOR US.

www.ingramcontent.com/pod-product-compliance
Lightning Source LLC
Chambersburg PA
CBHW080927050426
42334CB00055B/2835